Crystal Healing

A Beginner's Guide to the Healing

Powers of Crystals

Table of Contents

Introduction 1

Chapter 1: What is Crystal Healing and How Did It Start? 2

Chapter 2: Why Use Crystals for Healing? 8

Chapter 3: Understanding the Color Frequencies of Crystals ... 13

Chapter 4: Various Healing Crystals and Their Uses 19

Chapter 5: How to Choose the Right Healing Crystals 33

Chapter 6: How to Cleanse and Charge Crystals 56

Chapter 7: How to Use Crystals for Healing 70

Conclusion 80

Introduction

You are probably aware that many enthusiasts recognize crystals, rocks, and stones for their healing properties. These crystals have purposes that go far beyond simply looking and feeling stylish. They are not just used for aesthetic reasons, but also for health and healing.

Crystals can emit subtle energy to heal the body, mind, emotions, and spirit. With that in mind, you can start choosing crystals, rocks, and stones not only based on their appearance but also on their healing benefits.

If you want to start using crystals for healing purposes, then you will find this book truly helpful. This book provides up-to-date information about crystal healing, detailing a wide variety of crystals as well as their uses. At the completion of this book, you'll know exactly how to use a variety of crystals to target areas of your mind and body that require healing. Let's begin!

Chapter 1: What is Crystal Healing and How Did It Start?

Crystal healing refers to an alternative form of medicine, which utilizes semiprecious stones and crystals, like opal, amethyst, and quartz, recognized for holding healing powers. Many of those who practice this alternative form of medicine believe that it is capable of providing several benefits, including boosting energy, preventing bad energy from penetrating you, releasing energy blockages, and transforming the aura of your body. It also aims to restore the balance of your body and mind.

One reason why crystals are used for healing purposes is that they have unchanging and stable energy patterns. Each one also has a distinctive energy field (resonance) and frequency. This is what makes the crystals work like tuning forks. They can help harmonize your body's unstable energy field, contributing to the healing process.

History of Crystal Healing

Crystals, minerals, and gems have existed on Earth for a long time already. Almost all ancient civilizations took advantage of them and used them to achieve emotional, spiritual, and physical balance. With that said, it is safe to say that crystal healing holds a colorful and interesting history.

Crystal healing was even mentioned by Plato when he discussed the lost city of Atlantis. According to him, Atlanteans used a wide range of crystals to read the minds of others and transmit their thoughts. The first historical reference of using crystals is of Ancient Sumerians incorporating them into their magic formulas.

Ancient Egyptians also contributed to the colorful history of crystal healing. They used stones and crystals, including but not limited to carnelian, lapis lazuli, clear quartz, and emerald, in creating their pieces of jewelry and amulets as they believed that they promoted health and protection. They even used chrysolite (now referred to as peridot and topaz) for purging evil spirits and fighting night terrors.

The use of crystals also became popular in Ancient Greece. A lot of the names given to crystals at present came from the language of ancient Greek. Crystal, for instance, was derived from its Greek counterpart, "krýstallos," which means ice. The Greeks, during this time, strongly believed that the original form of clear quartz was water. It just froze excessively to the point that it could no longer go back to its liquid form, meaning it would stay solid forever.

They also wore amulets with amethyst, as they believed this stone could help prevent hangovers and drunkenness. The reason? Amethyst has a counterpart in the Greek language, which means "not drunken." Another example is hematite, which also came from a Greek word, meaning blood, since it tends to produce red coloration when it oxidizes.

Many Greek soldiers even had the habit of rubbing their bodies with ground hematite before their battles, as they strongly believed that it could help them become invincible. The Romans also wore talismans and amulets with crystals in them whenever they need protection from battles. They had a strong faith in the ability of the crystals to improve their health and attract positivity and good things.

Ancient China also contributed to the popularity of crystals. The ancient Chinese favored jade as a healing stone, as they strongly believed in its ability to heal kidney problems. The color of jade was also said to generate luck and fortune.

Crystal Healing During the Middle Ages

The popularity of crystals as a way to heal continued until the Middle Ages. In fact, these crystals played a major role in Christianity. Christians even viewed lapis lazuli, specifically, as a symbol of the Virgin Mary's purity. You can even see depictions of her wearing a ring made of sapphire starting around the 12th century.

During the Renaissance (around the 10th to 11th centuries), people used healing stones as natural remedies for those who were battling ailments. The Bishop of Rennes, France Marbode, even made documented observations regarding the power of precious stones to heal. You can see these documentations in Lapidary, which was published in 1539.

Another important part of the history of crystals and gemstones is when they were used by the native inhabitants of Australia, known as the Aborigines. The most commonly used ones were the quartz crystals. The aborigines made use of them as a means of connecting with spirits.

Crystal Healing Now

Crystals and gemstones were not only popular during the ancient periods. You can also see them being used today! They really regained their popularity during the 80s, the time when the New Age movement started. Even though crystal healing was a common form of therapy, it was not openly discussed during that period.

Despite that, new age crystal healing still had ties to three popular cultures – the Native American, Indian, and British cultures. The British culture took pride in its Pagan history that inspired many people to practice modern-day witchcraft. On the other hand, Indians took advantage of the power of crystals and incorporated them into a holistic healing approach. Indians even put this healing approach in their culture's holy texts.

As for the Western world, new-age crystal healing has a strong connection with the British culture, particularly paganism. There has been a resurgence of simplified versions of several ancient practices and rituals. This made crystal healing more accessible to Western society, with many people finding the ancient rituals appealing.

In Western astrology, you can see crystals being used and tied to modern paganism. Most of its practitioners believe that specific stones are in alignment with and share the same properties as specific planets. It is now even possible for you to use your astrological charts along with certain stones that perfectly suit the signs of your stars.

Crystals and precious stones are now finally being recognized for their contributions to natural and alternative healing. In countries and places that speak English, crystal healing has a strong association with the New Age's spiritual movement. Most of those who participate in crystal healing perceive it as an individuated practice, which strongly depends on creative expression and extreme personalization. Crystal healing practitioners also imply that crystals and stones have specific physical properties, like markings, shapes, and colors, which help identify the ailments that they can heal specifically.

Most practitioners choose crystals or stones for healing based on their colors and their perceived metaphysical qualities. They often put the chosen stones on certain body parts, with the placement and color selection being conducted based on concepts linked to chakras, energy grids, and grounding.

Crystal healing is also often featured in pieces of jewelry. Many even use them along with mindfulness, yoga, and meditation. It is no longer surprising to see crystal healing being used by different people of various social classes, with more and more people turning to this form of healing every day!

Chapter 2: Why Use Crystals for Healing?

All things surrounding humans emit a form of energy, and one way to connect with such energies, comprehend them, and heal from them is to use crystals. Many believe that crystals have tangible connections to the Earth's natural energy and elements.

Gemstones and crystals are already pure and pleasing aesthetically, but you can expect their real beauty to be derived from their cleansing and healing properties. These properties are what you can tap in order to take advantage of alternative healing.

The good thing about crystals is that aside from their beneficial properties, is that they are accessible to everyone. Crystals provide a variety of benefits safely, without causing side effects or stealing any energy.

Aside from healing specific ailments, crystals also help in re-energizing the body. They do so by releasing any energy blocks in your body. Crystals aren't only for physical healing either. They can be used to enhance your emotional, mental, and psychosomatic health. Listed below are a few of the incredible benefits you can expect to experience through using crystals:

- **Speeds Up Recovery** – You can expect crystals to help if you want to recover from an illness, injury, or any disruption in the energy flow of your body quickly. Through crystal healing, you can boost your emotional calmness and confidence, allowing you to heal your physical, mental, spiritual, and emotional problems.

- **Boosts Immunity** – Crystals also help in strengthening and boosting your immunity. Moreover, they can regulate your heartbeat and body rhythm. They can also strengthen your muscles.

- **Offers Relief Against Stress and Anxiety** – being free from extreme stress and anxiety can contribute greatly to improving your overall health.

- **Allows You to Take Advantage of Long-Lasting Relaxation** – You will feel more relaxed whenever you use crystals for healing. With that, it is also possible for such crystals to promote emotional healing.

- **Boosts Your Confidence**– Through crystal healing, you can gain more confidence in yourself, which encourages you to express yourself authentically.

While crystals can be used to heal physical ailments, it is safe to say that the majority of benefits of crystal healing focus more on areas surrounding your mental wellbeing. These include your feelings of positivity, peacefulness, and focus. Each crystal is recognized for its own unique and special properties that are in line with various areas of your life. The color, shape, and type of each crystal can strongly impact the benefits it provides.

Crystal Healing as a Vibrational Medicine

Many consider crystal healing a type of vibrational medicine because it uses vibrational frequencies when it comes to restoring or maintaining your health and wellness. Note that each area of your mind, body, and spirit holds an energy frequency. This energy frequency can either be healthy or unhealthy.

You need to keep these frequencies in perfect harmony if you want to achieve balance and improve your physical, mental, and emotional health. The problem is that there are times when you will experience an imbalance in such energies. Such an imbalance may cause you to become ill, whether it be physically, emotionally, or mentally.

As a vibrational medicine modality, crystal healing aims to restore the balance of your energy frequencies, leading to a significant improvement in your health. This form of vibrational healing occurs when the stone or crystal's energy frequency comes in contact with your own frequency. It could be the frequency of a body part or organ that you think needs healing.

You can expect both energy fields to interact, allowing the frequency of the crystal to rebalance the energy in your body. For instance, if you often suffer from a headache, then you can put amethyst on top of the specific spot where you experience the pain. This lets the crystal's energy flow to your painful, imbalanced area.

This results in restoring it to the right frequency. What is even better about crystal healing is that you can apply it to a wide variety of aspects of your life.

How Does it Work?

Crystal healing works specifically based on the overall composition and structure of each crystal. As mentioned earlier, crystals bring out vibrations at fixed frequencies (in other words, such vibrations are unchangeable). This makes crystals powerful as their physical contact with lower vibrations may increase your own vibrations as well as those around you.

Each time a crystal connects with your energy or body physically, you can expect it to attune you to the higher frequency known only to that crystal. With that, expect to be able to move beyond your physical, spiritual, and mental blockages.

Chapter 3: Understanding the Color Frequencies of Crystals

Before you start using crystals for healing, you should remember that there are thousands of them. It's important to learn more about the healing crystals you can use and their individual powers first, so you can make the most out of them.

One way to understand how powerful crystals are is to understand their individual color properties. Note that each crystal has a color frequency, which also has a psychological effect on you. Let us take, for example, citrine. This clear crystal with a tinge of yellow works as an effective pick-me-up for a lot of users. It can lift you mentally and emotionally. It could be due to the tinge of yellow in the crystal, which is known for encouraging a sunnier and more positive disposition.

To let you better understand the color frequencies of crystals, here are just a few of the most common ones and their associated healing capabilities:

Pink

Crystals that hold even just a hint of pink can give you a calming feeling, along with a gentle push of motivation. An example would be rose quartz, which has a reassuring and calming effect. It can also help release unwanted and unexpressed emotions that may be hampering your personal growth.

Red

Red crystals have the advantage of energizing, activating, and stimulating you. Crystals with this shade are often linked to your ability to utilize your practical and physical survival skills. A great example of a red crystal is ruby. This specific crystal works together with your heart chakra and helps to balance its energy.

Yellow

Yellow is also another color frequency that is significant for many healing crystals. Crystals that are kind of yellowish are strongly linked to your immune, digestive, and nervous systems' functions. You can even see contentment, happiness, fear, and stress being connected to this color.

A great example of a crystal that incorporates yellow is amber. It is beneficial not only for your nervous system but also for promoting the self-healing process. Another example is the citrine quartz crystal, which can clear your mind and improve your focus.

Orange

There are also orange crystals that have both focusing and energizing qualities. With such qualities around, your artistic and creative skills will emerge. One popular orange stone is carnelian, known for its warmth, which boosts your energy, motivation, and enthusiasm. It can also help you to become aware of your self-worth.

Green

Crystals with a touch of green have a strong connection to the human heart. With that, expect their frequencies to focus more on balancing relationships and emotions while promoting calmness, personal growth, and space. For instance, green aventurine effectively balances the heart by reducing emotional stress. Malachite tends to bring out all your concealed feelings, including resentment and hurt.

Light Blue

Another color frequency you have to familiarize yourself with as far as healing crystals are concerned is light blue. This color has a strong link to your throat, which is why it also focuses on communication. It prioritizes smell, sight, taste, and voice – basically all of your senses. It also encompasses internal communication – for instance, your self-talk, ability to express yourself, and thoughts.

Indigo

Crystals with this shade have a strong connection to the third eye. With that said, it is not surprising that a lot of people use indigo crystals to improve their perception, ability to understand, and intuition. Peace and quiet are also relevant to indigo. For instance, azurite encourages recall and memory. It can also free up any long-standing and challenging blocks in the way you communicate with others. Moreover, it can reveal the specific hindrances and blockages that tend to cause you to fail to reach your full potential.

Violet

Violet crystals have energies and frequencies that tend to tap into your willingness to serve others. This means that this color focuses more on empathy, inspiration, and imagination. This specific color frequency also aims to rebalance the extremes within your body systems. An example would be Amethyst, known to have universal benefits and uses. For one, you can use it to calm your mind during meditation. Moreover, this crystal also works in boosting your psychic powers and intuition.

White

You can also find clear and/or white crystals. This color represents the ability to reflect every energy surrounding you. It also symbolizes clarity, purification, and cleansing. Clear quartz, for instance, is great for those who intend to strengthen their energy. It is effective when it comes to channeling universal energy and absorbing, amplifying, transmitting, and balancing energy. With that, it is a great crystal to use in healing, meditation, and manifesting.

Black

Contrary to white, which aims to clarify and reflect light, black crystals and stones tend to focus more on the absorption of light. This also means that while white works in reflecting what is visible, black, on the other hand, aims to display the concealed potential of all situations you are in.

This color frequency is more focused on manifesting and solidifying. It is also grounding. One more thing that you should be aware of regarding this color frequency is that it quietly holds every energy within itself.

If you want to make the most out of crystals when it comes to healing, you should know the roles played by color in your daily life. Aside from infusing you with beauty and vibrancy, these color frequencies also play vital roles in healing. You can use them to achieve your optimum potential, whether mentally, physically, spiritually, or emotionally.

Chapter 4: Various Healing Crystals and Their Uses

As you now know, stones and crystals have their own distinctive energetic and metaphysical properties. These recognized energies and properties are the reasons they have been used for several centuries to increase abundance, prosperity, peace, and to treat a wide range of illnesses.

With the energetic healing capacities, emotional properties, and wisdom of these crystals and stones, you can expect them to influence your physical, intellectual, emotional, and spiritual body. Now, the question is, what are the most useful healing crystals. Let's talk about a few examples of the best healing crystals that you can use right now, and the specific areas and aspects of your health and overall wellbeing that they target.

Amethyst

Amethyst is a famous healing crystal recognized for its ability to bring tranquility and peace to any home. It has healing, purifying, and protective properties that help remove negative thoughts while replenishing your body. It is believed to encourage spiritual wisdom, sincerity, and humility.

With the many benefits offered by Amethyst, it shouldn't be surprising to see it as one of the most commonly used stones in the New Age. The fact that you can also easily find it in different parts of the world also makes it even more popular. Known for its beautiful purple shade, it can do many things, though it seems to be best known for manifestation.

Metaphysical Healing Benefits

You can use amethyst to connect with your ultimate purpose in life as well as the real desires of your heart. You can then manifest these desires with the help of amethyst. Linked to the upper chakra, amethyst also works in bringing the ethereal to the physical realm. For instance, it can help you make your earthly dreams come true.

Physical Healing Benefits

If you intend to use amethyst for physical healing, then be aware that one of the areas of your body it can target is your sympathetic nervous system. It is also a big help in balancing hormones, easing and relieving headaches and neck tension, and curing insomnia.

It is a great companion every time you go to bed as it lets you sleep peacefully, aids with your sleeping problems, and decodes dreams. One simple way to achieve such a benefit is to put it beneath your pillow every night. It will let you sleep deeply and wake up fully rested, making you fully prepared to manifest and take on whatever challenges you may encounter during the day.

Citrine

Citrine is a kind of quartz known for its golden-yellow shade. Based on its color, you can connect this crystal with optimism and joy. Many also refer to it as the money stone as it helps manifest wealth, abundance, and prosperity. Citrine can get rid of negative traits, such as fear, and promote clarity and motivation. It can also boost the energies of other stones and crystals surrounding it.

Metaphysical Healing Benefits

You can carry citrine every time you need to perform an activity that involves money and finances. For instance, you may bring it with you whenever you visit the bank or attend business meetings that focus on your finances. You can also put this crystal on your desk and look at it every time you work. Doing so can help in attracting financial stability, wealth, and abundance.

Physical Healing Benefits

As far as your physical body and health and wellness are concerned, citrine has a wide range of uses. For one, it can stimulate your metabolism. It is also a big help if you are frequently dealing with nausea and digestion problems. Moreover, it contributes a lot to strengthening your nerve impulses, which is actually good for your brain as it helps you to think sharply and quickly.

Turquoise

Recognized for being a real master healer, turquoise is a stone you should carry around. It is famous for its ability to act as the energetic bridge between heaven and earth. Ever since healing crystals became popular, this blue stone has been recognized for its benefits, particularly its lucky and protective properties.

Moreover, turquoise is valued for symbolizing wisdom, and is represented as such in various ancient cultures. It was one of the most cherished stones by kings, shamans, chiefs, and wizards.

Metaphysical Healing Benefits

One of the metaphysical healing benefits of turquoise is that it can strengthen your body's meridians. It can also offer support to your intuition and allow you to meditate in peace. The fact that it has a blue shade makes it easily identifiable with the throat chakra.

With such an association, it is safe to say that it is a major contributor to help you improve how you communicate with others. You can carry this with you in the form of a talisman, so you will be protected by its protective properties. Carrying it with you also works in channeling its emitted ancient wisdom.

Physical Healing Benefits

In terms of physical healing, turquoise can target problems affecting your brain, throat, ears, and neck. It also has a strong connection with the psychic realm. It is an incredible stone to use if you want to get rid of energy blockages. It can also contribute to ensuring that there is a healthy and smooth flow of energy throughout your body.

Rose Quartz

This is a healing crystal, which greatly symbolizes unconditional love. Many even refer to it as the love stone. It has an attractive pink shade, a color that one can immediately associate with the heart. You can use it to express your unconditional love not only to others but also to yourself, the planet, and the things surrounding you.

Metaphysical Healing Benefits

Rose quartz is indeed an incredible stone that you can use to invite and encourage love. You will find it useful in sharing your love with others and attracting your soulmate. With that said, it is safe to assume that rose quartz mainly focuses on the heart. You can carry or wear this stone to help open yourself up to the idea of finding love, especially if you are still single. You can also use it in nurturing and deepening your love, just in case you are already in a romantic relationship.

Physical Healing Benefits

With its focus on your heart chakra, you will surely find rose quartz useful when dealing with deep emotional healing and release. It can also contribute towards improving your blood circulation and keeping your blood pressure low. Many crystal healing practitioners and proponents agree that rose quartz is effective in easing palpitations, irregular or skipping heartbeats, and releasing tension.

Lapis Lazuli

As one of the most ancient healing crystals ever used, lapis lazuli is a beautiful crystal with a blue hue known for its high energy vibrations. Having such high vibrations is why this crystal is so appealing to anyone who wants to speed up their spiritual growth.

No, it will not be able to provide you with a magical shortcut towards attaining enlightenment, but it can certainly provide you with the kind of receptiveness that will let you open yourself up to divine guidance. Lapis lazuli is also strongly connected with luxury and royalty. It has celestial properties that guide you in ensuring that you can do your activities with good judgment and wisdom.

Metaphysical Healing Benefits

Lapis lazuli is recognized for its ability to activate your ethereal upper chakra. It is also the crystal used for empowering your throat chakra to promote clear communication while also letting you express your ideas freely and easily. It is an intriguing stone, which promotes truth and internal observation while assisting you in discovering and representing the spiritual world.

Physical Healing Benefits

Lapis lazuli is also very powerful and beneficial as far as physical healing is concerned. It is the stone you need to heal and support your vocal cords, throat, and larynx. It also has a very strong connection with the brain. With that, you can also expect it to relieve ADD (attention deficit disorder). It does so by improving your mental focus and getting rid of unwanted and unnecessary thoughts.

Moonstone

Famous for its light blue and translucent shade, the moonstone is a healing crystal that is easily accessible in different parts of the world. It has strong connections to feminine lunar energy. It is also the ideal stone to use if you want to cultivate internal harmony while strengthening your intuition. Recognized for being regal and sacred, it should come as no surprise that it is regarded as being the stone of ancient gods and goddesses in India.

Metaphysical Healing Benefits

You can expect moonstone to work in opening you up so you can get in touch with other worlds as well as the universe. It is also useful in combating materialism and regulating and managing your ego.

Physical Healing Benefits

Moonstone is also good for your physical health as it can support your digestive system and pituitary gland. It is also helpful in preventing obesity. Other health issues that moonstone can heal are hormonal problems, water retention, and menstrual problems.

Aventurine

Aventurine is also another healing crystal, which is closely linked to your heart chakra. The energies it emits can encourage you to follow what your heart tells you, bravely. It can also amplify your luck, abundance, and prosperity. Moreover, it is a crystal that can help attract new opportunities.

Metaphysical Healing Benefits

With its strong connection to the heart chakra, aventurine is a big help if your goal is to create emotional calmness and a sense of wellbeing. It is what you need to keep your emotional, physical, and mental health in harmony. Also, it works in reestablishing balance.

Physical Healing Benefits

When it comes to your physical health, aventurine is also a positive contributor. It supports the good health of your heart and ensures that energy and blood circulate smoothly and healthily. Aventurine is also said to contribute to speeding up your recovery from an illness, surgery, and injury.

Other Stones and Crystals Recognized for Their Healing Properties

Apart from the ones already mentioned, you can also use any of the following stones and crystals for your crystal healing sessions as they are also well known for their healing powers and properties:

- **Jade** – This stone is famous for holding energies of tranquility and purity. It is what you need to feel calm and at peace. It also contributes to the good health of your adrenal glands and in relieving headaches.

- **Garnet** – This can help heal your root chakra. You will also find this gem helpful in relieving sciatica and back pain. Aside from that, it can balance calcium deficiency and aid in effective tissue regeneration.

- **Topaz** – You can also use topaz if your goal is to achieve hormonal balance or fight the aging process. The fact that topaz vibrates together with the energies emitted by your throat chakra also means that it is a major contributor to expressing yourself. It also promotes clear communication and heals problems linked to your voice, neck, and throat.

- **Sapphire** – This blue stone represents royalty and wisdom. It attracts peace, happiness, and prosperity.

When it comes to physical healing, it can assist in curing eye issues and blood disorders. It also works on cellular levels and relieves anxiety, insomnia, and depression.

- **Clear Quartz** – Clear quartz holds the title of the master healer for several good reasons. One is that it is effective in amplifying positive energy and thought. It works in storing, releasing, regulating, and absorbing energy. It can also improve your psychic ability, unlock your memory, and improve your concentration. Furthermore, it is a great stone to use to improve your immunity and restore balance to your body.

- **Hematite** – This crystal can absorb toxic emotions that may block you from achieving genuine happiness and natural vitality. You can use this crystal in removing negative feelings, particularly those that cause anxiety, worry, and stress.

- **Tiger's Eye** – This one is famous for providing relief against the early warning signs of asthma. It also alleviates headaches. Furthermore, it is good for your digestive system as it contributes to its proper function.

- **Black Tourmaline** – You can also use black tourmaline if your goal is to find immediate relief from various forms of body pains. It can strengthen your immune system, too. Apart from that, it could be a big help in healing problems linked to your adrenal glands, legs, spinal column, and kidneys.

• **Fluorite** – One great advantage of this crystal is that it boosts your concentration and focus to the point that you can achieve mental clarity. It is, therefore, an effective protector and healer.

• **Aquamarine** – You should use aquamarine in your crystal healing sessions, especially if your goal is to restore or maintain the beauty and vibrancy of youth. The reason is that aquamarine contains plenty of fantastic anti-aging properties. It has soothing energy, making it an effective crystal to help calm fears and deal with phobias.

• **Kyanite** – With its calming blue-green color, you can easily associate Kyanite with the sky, so expect it to be very soothing to your nerves. It is one of the best crystals to use when it comes to healing pain affecting your throat. You can also use it in improving communication. Moreover, kyanite works in easing headaches, tension, and eye pain.

• **Opal** – Opal is a colorful stone closely connected to the eye, particularly the third eye chakra. You will find opal useful in supporting eye health and improving your vision. It is also effective in stabilizing neurotransmitter disturbances and stimulating memory. Furthermore, it can inspire happiness, appreciation, and optimism.

Mentioned in this chapter are just some of the many stones and crystals you can use for crystal healing. There are of course many more to choose from, but the ones discussed here are a great place to begin your crystal healing efforts.

Chapter 5: How to Choose the Right Healing Crystals

For beginners, picking the right crystals to use for healing purposes can be quite overwhelming – what with the numerous choices laid out to them. Apart from those mentioned in the previous chapter, you can find thousands of other gemstones and crystals, each having their own unique structure, use, color, and energy. It is crucial that you know exactly what your purpose or intention will be, as this will be key in selecting the right crystals for you.

You can choose a crystal based either on your intuition or your intention. You can allow your intuition to guide you if you are still unsure of what you intend to focus on. In that case, you can pick your healing stones by feeling or looking at your different options until you get drawn to at least one of them.

While you may think that you are the one who picks the crystals, it is usually the crystal that chooses you. It captures your attention through its dazzling colors, patterns, and shapes. Also, with each crystal's distinctive vibrational energy, your intuition will effectively guide you towards the stones and crystals that are most suitable for you based on a particular moment in your life.

Another way to pick a crystal is to match it with your intentions. For instance, if you intend to pick a crystal to improve your overall well-being, you must determine a specific challenge or problem you are presently facing.

After deciding on a specific intention or goal, you can finally match it with a crystal that emits energy capable of supporting such an intention or goal. For instance, if your intention is to manifest abundance in your life, you could choose citrine, which is powerful in manifesting such desires.

How to Craft Your Intention

Learning about what intention is specifically and how you can craft one is the key to selecting the most suitable crystals and stones for you. In this case, you should remind yourself that thoughts can create vibrations throughout the universe. With that said, the act of setting intentions will always serve as an incredible and powerful tool to achieve happiness and well-being.

Your intention will give you with a clear purpose in life. It is what will provide you a clear insight into your values, dreams, and aspirations. It is also like a magnet in the sense that it attracts the things that can help it come true. With that in mind, you should start crafting and setting your intention by setting your goals first, particularly those capable of aligning you with your purpose, aspirations, and values.

Determining and setting your intention can be made easier by following these tips:

- **Determine What Truly Matters to You** – Note that your values serve as driving forces of your life. Determine what matters to you the most, especially if you wish to achieve happiness and fulfillment.

- **Find Areas and Aspects of Your Life That Require an Upgrade** – Determine the specific areas where you think you can improve your career, health, community, social life, relationships, and spirituality.

- **Be Specific** – Make sure that you are specific on the things you wish to achieve. You also have to determine the specific time you intend to achieve it and your exact reasons.

- **Make Your Intentions Come to Life** – One way to do so is to put your intention to writing. When doing so, make sure that you use the present tense. It should be like your intention is happening right now. You then need to affirm the specific intention or goal you want. Put your target goal in writing, too. It should be the end result you intend to achieve from what you are manifesting.

You need to be patient while quieting your mind and figuring out what will work for you specifically. An effective way of testing various crystals is holding the stone while thinking quietly of your exact intention.

Observe the sensations you feel. You may feel pulsations, tranquility, calmness, and warmth or coldness. All these could be signs that the stone is ideal for the kind of healing you intend to achieve. The reason is that it emits unique energy vibrations that interact with the vibrations that you produce on your own. This can have a direct impact on your subtle, emotional, and physical body.

Choose the Right Crystal Based on a Chakra

Apart from using either your intuition or intention, you can also pick the right crystal that you can use for healing based on which one resonates perfectly with a certain chakra. If you are still unfamiliar with chakras, note that they refer to spiritual energy centers usually portrayed as spinning wheels. Opening your chakras is the key to keeping you healthy and balanced.

If a particular chakra is unbalanced or blocked, you will likely experience problems in various aspects of your life. In this case, you can take advantage of stones and crystals as they can help heal any blockage or imbalance in your chakras.

There are seven primary chakras, with all of them aligning with your spine through to the top of your head. All your chakras are also connected to your major organs and nervous systems and your spiritual, psychological, and emotional being. Every chakra has a stone and color associated with it, too.

With that in mind, you have to identify the specific chakra you intend to balance or unblock first, so you can figure out the specific crystal that can help you. Here are the seven primary chakras that you have to be aware of. Indicated in this section are also some of the crystals strongly connected to them.

Base/Root Chakra

The color assigned to the base chakra is red. With this chakra, you can ground your energy together with the Earth. Situated at your spine's base, this chakra is strongly connected with security and survival. Among the crystals resonating with this chakra are bloodstone, hematite, red jasper, and black tourmaline, so consider picking any of them if it is what you intend to heal.

Sacral Chakra

With orange as its assigned color, you can expect the sacral chakra to assist in letting the vital energy flow smoothly through your body. This chakra is positioned beneath your stomach or belly button. Your sacral chakra is also recognized for being the center of one's emotions, creativity, sexual organs, and pleasure. If this is the chakra you intend to clear, balance, or open up, then you may want to use amber, sunstone, orange calcite, and/or carnelian during your crystal healing session.

Solar Plexus Chakra

The solar plexus is a great-looking chakra in the shade of yellow. It is specifically connected with your neural network. This chakra's main focus is self-confidence and personal power, which is why it contributes to showing your true self without any reservations and judgment. Located just beneath your breastbone, this specific chakra is one that you can activate with crystals that resonate with it, including pyrite, yellow jasper, citrine, and rutilated quartz.

Heart Chakra

With the colors pink and green representing the heart chakra, you can expect it to emanate unconditional love, forgiveness, and compassion. You can see this chakra at the center of your chest. This chakra connects the lower physical chakras to the higher chakras that are of a more spiritual nature. If you wish to target your heart chakra, then you should pick stones and crystals that nicely resonate with it – among which are green jade, green aventurine, rose quartz, and emerald.

Throat Chakra

Sky blue is the color of the throat chakra, which is recognized for being the center of self-expression and communication. You can find this chakra at your neck's base. It is one of the chakras positioned in the higher parts of your body, signifying its spiritual nature. Crystals that resonate with the throat chakra are lapis lazuli, aquamarine, blue apatite, and turquoise.

Third Eye Chakra

Represented by its deep indigo color, the third eye chakra acts as the center of your intuition. It is necessary to stimulate it if you want to improve your psychic ability and activate your pineal gland. For that purpose, you can use labradorite, amethyst, purple fluorite, and shungite.

Crown Chakra

The color of the crown chakra could be white or violet. It is a mystical chakra strongly connected to your higher consciousness, particularly your destiny and divine purpose. As the crown chakra, it is positioned on the top of your head. A few examples of stones and crystals that tend to resonate with the crown chakra are diamond, amethyst, selenite, and clear quartz.

For you to pick a crystal strongly connected to a specific chakra, it is advisable to spend time examining the character, color, and energy of the crystal and how it tends to resonate with you. Note that several crystals are related to each chakra but have qualities and properties that align with more than one chakra. Be sure to keep that in mind when making your choice.

Choosing the Right Crystal Based on Astrology

Another method of picking a crystal that you can use for healing purposes is to base it on your zodiac or astrological sign. This method is ideal, especially if you have no focus or intention in mind yet. In this case, you have to determine what your zodiac or astrological sign is based on your birth date.

Here are the 12 astrological/zodiac signs and the specific stones and crystals that work well with them:

Stones and Crystals for Aries

Ruby *(Color – Red / Chakra – Root, Heart)* – Supports the strong leadership traits and passion of Aries, and counters its negative traits, including the tendency to lose motivation fast, restlessness, and impulsiveness. It can also restore courage and confidence, especially when dealing with challenging tasks.

Carnelian *(Color – Red and Orange / Chakra – Sacral, Root)* – This is the best stone for an Aries with doubts about his/her capacities. It can improve self-worth and confidence as well as problem-solving skills.

Snow Quartz *(Color – White / Chakra – Crown)* – Ideal for use when an Aries finds things too overwhelming. With its soft feminine energy, it can efficiently balance yin-yang energies and chakras. It can open a connection to supreme consciousness while helping one find a balance between sticking to a healthy workload and fulfilling responsibilities.

Red Jasper *(Color – Red / Chakra – Root, Sacral)* – This can deal with the impulsiveness of an Aries. With its grounding energy, red jasper can stimulate a more calculated response and encourage patience.

Stones and Crystals for Taurus

Emerald *(Color – Green / Chakra – Heart)* – Encourages a Taurus to be more patient and loyal. You can also use it for healing whenever you feel like you are not that secure in your romantic or professional relationship, which is a typical Taurus feeling. It also compliments the love of Taurus' for financial acumen and luxury.

Blue Kyanite *(Color – Blue with White Streaks / Chakra – Third Eye, Throat)* – Inspires you to express your beliefs and opinions. Its high vibrations can enhance a Taurus' awareness, mental thought, and intuitive abilities. It is a great help whenever a Taurus deals with difficult and challenging people or is reluctant in expressing himself due to fear that he might upset someone.

Rose Quartz *(Color – Pink / Chakra – Heart)* – It can balance a Taurus' heart chakra, making it possible to open up the heart to loved ones, romantic partners, friends, and oneself. It also works in soothing any feelings of inadequacy, often resulting from the overprotectiveness and excessive jealousy of a Taurus.

Peridot *(Color – Green / Chakra – Solar Plexus, Heart)* – Gets rid of negative traits that are so typical in a Taurus, particularly those that prevent you from reaching your dreams. It is typical for a Taurus to hold himself back due to rigid and strict beliefs, jealousy, and fear of change. With the light energy of peridot, it is possible to bring a more positive perspective, thereby allowing a Taurus to overcome jealousy and emotional blocks.

Stones and Crystals for Gemini

Agate *(Colors - Blue, Green, Brown, Red, White, Yellow / Chakra – Base, Heart)* – A powerful crystal for Geminis that further enhances their love for learning and intelligent conversations. It also has a kind of magnetism that retains a Gemini's focus, especially because those born under this sign have the tendency to get bored and a bit nosy now and then.

Celestite *(Color – Blue / Chakra – Throat, Crown)* – An incredible gemstone to enhance the strengths of a Gemini, which is mainly communication. It can also fight this zodiac sign's negative traits, including nervousness, indecision, and the tendency to be at a loss for words. It has soothing energy capable of easing worries and stimulating mental clarity.

Howlite *(Color – White, Green / Chakra – Crown, Heart)* – Effective in balancing spiritual centers, making it possible for a Gemini to bring out their positive traits, including being naturally sociable, fun-loving, and energetic. It can also prevent a Gemini's chakras from becoming imbalanced, thereby ensuring that you do not turn your spontaneity into impulsiveness and restlessness.

Serpentine *(Color – Red, Brown, Brown-Yellow, Brown-Red / Chakra – Crown)* – Stimulates a Gemini's crown chakra, which is good for promoting mental and nervous calmness and better intuition. It can also make a Gemini proudly and confidently stand up for herself instead of letting outside pressures get to her.

Stones and Crystals for Cancer

Moonstone (Color – Yellow Milky Sheen, Cream, White / Chakra – Crown) – Lets you go with the flow of the constantly changing rhythms of life. This makes it useful for those born under the sign of Cancer who seem to be afraid of taking risks. It can also stabilize emotions, which is good as Cancerians also tend to have mood swings and fluctuations.

Ruby *(Color – Red / Chakra – Root, Heart)* – Balances your temperament and ensures that the insecurity and fear that are typical for Cancerians will not prevent them from reaching their goals. Ruby can emit energy capable of stimulating a Cancer's motivation and passion.

Opal *(Color – Colorless, Pink, Blue, Black, White, Green, Yellow / Chakra – Throat, Crown, Heart)* – Promotes emotional balance, allowing Cancerians to go deep into their emotions and stop past events and resentments from holding them back.

Emerald *(Color – Green / Chakra – Heart)* – Strengthens memory and promotes truthfulness, especially with yourself. It encourages unity and loyalty in a relationship. It can also deal with the short-tempered nature of Cancerians as it aids in developing their patience.

Stones and Crystals for Leo

Golden Yellow Topaz *(Color - Golden Yellow / Chakra – Sacral, Solar Plexus)* – Amplifies Leo's intentions, making it possible to manifest almost anything, especially for those that are spiritual in nature. This crystal also helps a Leo become successful by recognizing their capacities and skills and their positive influence towards others. It also elevates one's energy, which is good because most of those born under Leo are sociable.

Hiddenite *(Color – Green / Chakra – Third Eye, Heart)* – A variation of kunzite, this stone is ideal for a Leo who usually faces difficulty releasing their feelings of failure. Someone born under the sign of Leo can also use Hiddenite to gain encouragement whenever they are dealing with challenges. It can support new beginnings while also helping a Leo develop truly meaningful relationships.

Citrine *(Color – Yellow / Chakra – Crown, Solar Plexus)* – For a Leo, citrine is a stone capable of boosting their energy. It can boost positivity and joy, even during those instances when insecurities strike. It is also the key to countering Leo's somewhat negative trait, which is oversensitivity when facing criticisms. If you are a Leo, then citrine can boost your confidence and improve your ability to accept constructive criticism gracefully.

Black Onyx *(Color – Black / Chakra – Root)* – Ideal for anyone born under the Leo sign; black onyx should be the go-to crystal for calming excessive energy. It can also contribute to overcoming self-doubt, which is quite common among Leos. This is all thanks to the stone's protective and grounding energy.

Stones and Crystals for Virgo

Green Jade *(Color – Green / Chakra – Heart)* – Encourages a Virgo to take responsibility for their own happiness, goals, and financial stability. It also aims to balance the emotional, mental, and physical areas of life, particularly those revolving around work, relationships, and family. It can also further boost attention to detail, a good trait of Virgos.

Blue Tourmaline *(Color – Blue / Chakra – Third Eye, Throat)* – Supports the natural desire of a Virgo to serve others. It also boosts the confidence of a Virgo and amplifies intuitive and psychic abilities. It supports living harmoniously with the environment.

Peridot *(Color – Green / Chakra – Solar Plexus, Heart)* – Assists a Virgo in overcoming life's roadblocks, like past mistakes, old baggage, and self-criticisms, thereby promoting quick progress to reaching goals. With its stress-relieving elements and properties, a Virgo can also benefit from using peridot, especially when dealing with too much stress.

Red Jasper *(Color – Red / Chakra – Sacral, Root)* – Brings comfort, wholeness, peace, and tranquility to the somewhat stressful life of a Virgo. It is very nurturing, plus it can improve problem-solving and organizational skills. It also helps a Virgo deal with their negative thoughts, sending a reminder to reconnect with this zodiac sign's earthy nature.

Stones and Crystals for Libra

Blue Sapphire *(Color – Blue / Chakra – Throat, Third Eye)* – An incredible stone that embodies balance, sincerity, and wisdom. It also helps a Libra deal with struggles linked to practicing self-discipline, allowing them to improve their focus and curb the habit of procrastination. Blue sapphire can also improve relationships and the loyalty and faithfulness usually valued by a Libra.

Rose Quartz *(Color – Pink / Chakra – Heart)* – Supports inner peace, good relationships, and self-love. This specific stone can reinforce self-worth, inspiring a Libra to see their inner beauty. It can also make a Libra realize that self-love can also lead to genuine happiness. Moreover, it can get rid of resentment and anger while easing any existing conflicts.

Ametrine *(Color – Yellow, Purple / Chakra – Solar Plexus, Crown)* – Encourages a Libra to trust their instincts, which is a great advantage as an inherent trait of this zodiac sign is indecisiveness. It also encourages committing to a plan or course of action, plus it can improve spiritual and mental clarity. Moreover, it can help battle prejudice and handle any imbalance with the yin-yang.

Lapis Lazuli *(Color – Deep Blue / Chakra – Third Eye, Throat)* – A great crystal for a Libra with its ability to represent freedom and power. It also brings out a sense of calmness and serenity. It provides the needed encouragement to voice out your opinions and thoughts. Moreover, it can establish a strong network composed of positive relationships, a great advantage for a Libra who does not usually favor the thought of being alone.

Stones and Crystals for Scorpio

Aquamarine *(Color – Green, Pale Blue / Chakra – Throat)* – Helps in resolving arguments and releasing anger, an advantage considering that Scorpios usually have a fiery temperament that can turn to hostility whenever provoked. Aquamarine can also support a Scorpio's intelligence and cultivate the confidence and courage needed to try a new endeavor.

Smoky Quartz *(Color – Brown, Light to Dark Grey / Chakra – Crown, Root)* – Releases emotional baggage and other bottled-up emotions, which is great for Scorpios as they tend to be sensitive and secretive. This crystal can also improve psychic abilities, allowing a Scorpio to reconnect with their intuitive abilities whenever they feel trapped in a specific situation.

Malachite *(Color – Green / Chakra – Throat, Heart)* – Supports the constantly changing energy of a Scorpio. Possessing the sign of water, Scorpios expect to experience constant movements, and malachite can offer protection throughout their journey. It could be when traveling, changing perceptions, or making a life-changing decision. It also helps a Scorpio take responsibility for all their actions.

Ruby *(Color – Red / Chakra – Root, Heart)* – Scorpios are famous for being passionate about many things, be it a relationship, project, or new beginnings. Therefore, the vibrant color of ruby resonates beautifully with such energy, thereby further boosting the Scorpio's courageous nature. This gemstone is also useful in firing up one's libido, deepening closeness in romantic relationships, and improving fertility.

Stones and Crystals for Sagittarius

Lapis Lazuli *(Color – Deep Blue / Chakra – Third Eye, Throat)* – Activates the third eye, encouraging truth and wisdom. It supports the love and desire of Sagittarius to explore spirituality and boost spiritual knowledge. It can also support the desire of the Sagittarius to embrace freedom and independence.

Blue Topaz *(Color – Blue / Chakra – Throat, Third Eye)* – Brings out a vibrational frequency that emits truth, a trait valued by a Sagittarius. Sometimes, Sagittarians struggle to express their emotions, a sign of an imbalance in the throat chakra. This is something that the blue topaz can deal with as it can stimulate the throat chakra, promoting balance in emotions. With that, it becomes easier to express emotions and opinions honestly and confidently.

Turquoise *(Color – Green, Blue / Chakra – Throat)* – Sagittarius has the inherent trait of wanting to lead. They are often quick thinkers, decisive, and independent, but if their chakras are no longer in proper alignment, they tend to become vain and self-absorbed, damaging relationships and hampering their chances of attaining success. By using turquoise, it is possible to realign and rebalance the chakras of a Sagittarius. This is a great way to balance their impulsiveness and selfishness with empathetic traits.

Wulfenite *(Color – Orange, Grey, Green, Yellow, Brown, White / Chakra – Sacral, Heart, Solar Plexus)* – The inherent generosity and kindness of Sagittarians make them prey to those who may take advantage of them. With the help of this birthstone, you can make proper judgments, allowing you to decide whether someone truly deserves your help. Wulfenite can also stimulate inspiration and creativity.

Stones and Crystals for Capricorn

Garnet *(Color – Pink, Deep Red, Clear Green, Brown, Orange / Chakra – Root)* – Stimulates charisma and optimism in a Capricorn with naturally pessimistic traits. It can also inspire loyalty, commitment, and devotion in a relationship. Moreover, garnet has activating energy capable of strengthening the survival instincts of a Capricorn.

Emerald *(Color – Green / Chakra – Heart)* – Symbolizes inner growth. It inspires the highest level of patience and loyalty, thereby keeping relationships balanced. It is also the crystal that a Capricorn needs whenever he/she is struggling with overwhelming emotions.

Malachite *(Color – Green / Chakra – Throat, Heart)* – This moonstone is a great help for any highly motivated Capricorn as it gives them the courage to take a risk and aim for quick and excellent results. It is also helpful in developing empathy.

Azurite *(Color – Blue / Chakra – Third Eye, Throat)* – Works effectively in opening up a Capricorn to divine guidance. It can improve your intuition by extending and complementing your supreme principles. Moreover, it inspires you to develop great ideas and improve your concentration and work ethics.

Stones and Crystals for Aquarius

Aquamarine *(Color – Green, Pale Blue / Chakra – Throat)* – Builds a connection to the heart center, which also aids in relieving stress, something that an Aquarian is vulnerable to.

Aquamarine also has cool and nice colors that can calm and quiet the mind, allowing you to achieve peace and clarity.

Magnetite *(Color – Grey, Brown, Black / Chakra – Root)* – Being inherently magnetic, magnetite is capable of both attracting and repelling energies. It can align the chakras of someone born under the sign of Aquarius, thereby promoting emotional stability. It is also effective in balancing opposite traits, like energizing someone while also encouraging relaxation.

Celestite *(Color – Blue / Chakra – Throat, Crown)* – Brings out a heavenly vibration, which can stimulate spiritual development while establishing a connection to the angelic realms. This is a big help for Aquarians since they tend to struggle with developing their spirituality. Celestite also has a softer influence that can make an Aquarian stay balanced and flexible.

Black Onyx *(Color – Black / Chakra – Root)* – This stone positively aligns with the energy and nature of an Aquarius. It has grounding and protective elements and properties capable of calming any excess energy. It also lessens anxiety and stress, which is common among Aquarians, as they also tend to overwork themselves while being overwhelmed by self-doubts.

Stones and Crystals for Pisces

Amethyst *(Color – Purple to Lavender / Chakra – Third Eye, Crown)* – Pisces has the inherent trait of wanting to escape from reality, making them prone to addiction, like smoking and alcoholism. Amethyst can help, in this case, as it can prevent overindulgence by strengthening resolve. It also helps in attaining inner peace and discovering the exact reasons for certain behaviors. With that, it becomes a lot easier to overcome unwanted habits.

Bloodstone *(Color – Green with Red Flecks / Chakra – Heart, Solar Plexus, Root, Sacral)* – Pisces are naturally sensitive, which is also the trait that can make them take on the problems of others as their own. With the help of bloodstone, you can remind yourself that your feelings and emotions are important, too. This can prevent you from focusing too much on others and forgetting about yourself.

Smithsonite *(Color – Green, Blue / Chakra – Throat)* – Radiates kindness and charm, which also works in balancing the emotions and lowering the stress level of anyone born under the Pisces astrological sign. It is also useful in improving the psychic strength of Pisces. It also promotes better communication and improves one's compassionate nature.

Fluorite *(Color – A Rainbow of Colors / Chakra – Third Eye, Throat, Heart)* – Helps a Piscean with an unbalanced or closed third eye, allowing them to deal with confusion or mental turmoil. The use of this crystal also works to boost mental focus and stimulate and balance the energy centers. It works in sharpening thoughts and allowing new and creative ideas to come to the mind.

Additional Tips for Choosing the Right Crystal

While there are several methods and ways for you to pick a crystal to use for healing purposes, remember that the most crucial piece of advice is to put your full trust in your intuition. Also, note that although there is no specific right or wrong method of choosing a crystal, it is still advisable for you to look for a connection.

Also, avoid worrying too much about making a poor choice. Remember that all gemstones and crystals possess an imprint of their energy and structure, so it is highly likely that any type of crystal will support whatever purpose or intention you have in mind – just some will be more effective than others. The thing you should tinker with is the vibration of the crystal and the way that it resonates with your own energy field.

Chapter 6: How to Cleanse and Charge Crystals

Once you have chosen the specific stones and crystals you intend to use for healing based on the methods mentioned in the previous chapter; the next step is to cleanse and charge them. You need to cleanse the crystals first before you can use them. By cleansing and charging them first, you can make the most out of them and bring out their optimum healing potential.

The Importance of Cleansing Healing Crystals

Healing crystals can benefit you in the sense that they can improve various aspects of your life, but before using them for healing, you should remind yourself that the energies they emit also get drained. The problem is that when such energies get depleted, there is a chance for unwanted and negative energies to replace them.

With that said, you have to cleanse the crystals and stones you have chosen before you ever start using them. It would even be much better if you also charge them. By ensuring that they are completely cleansed and charged, you can prevent negative energies from building up in your chosen crystals that may negatively influence not only you but also those around you. Cleansing is also crucial in ensuring that the energy will remain pure and positive.

Cleansing is all about getting rid of all the unwanted energies that the crystal or stone has absorbed, bringing back its clean and pure form. It is different from charging crystals, which is about replenishing their healing energy after depletion. Cleansing, therefore, should come first before you do the charging of crystals.

So basically, you need to cleanse and charge stones and crystals in these situations:

- After buying them

- Before and after using them for healing purposes

- After exposing them to negative energies – Examples include arguments, chaos, and heavy emotions

- After being handled by other people

Ways to Purify and Cleanse Healing Crystals

As mentioned earlier, cleansing the crystals is necessary for restoring their vibrational and real energy. The good thing about cleansing is that it also helps nurture your relationship with your chosen crystals.

When it comes to cleansing, though, you should remember that you can't expect all crystals to have similar responses to a particular cleansing method. You can also find some recharging and cleansing techniques that work and resonate better with a particular crystal. With that said, you have to choose a method based on the stones and crystals you intend to use.

Here are a couple of options for cleansing methods and the basic steps involved in using them:

Sunlight Cleanse

This cleansing method is perfect if you are looking for a natural yet powerful approach. However, you should avoid overdoing it as it may lead to unwanted results. Make sure to limit the exposure to the sun to at most thirty minutes. You can use this cleansing method with any stone and crystal, provided you stick to the recommended duration.

If you expose them to the sun for longer than half an hour, then it is likely that some stones and crystals will begin to fade – among which are amethyst, aquamarine, citrine, quartz, opal, topaz, fluorite, turquoise, and sapphire.

Using direct sunlight at the recommended duration can help light pass through each crystal and make it act like sandpaper, or a comb. To do the sunlight cleanse, here are the usual steps:

- Look for an area outdoors that receives sunlight.

- Prepare this space by putting sacred intentions, mindfulness, incense, candles, and any other ceremonial practices that resonate with you.

- Once ready, set your chosen stones or crystals in the designated spot. Let them stay there for a max of thirty minutes. This should be enough time to let them soak up the light's sacred vibrations. During this time, try to become more conscious of the words you say and your thoughts. The reason is that the cleansing period is the time when you will also impart all your energy to the crystal.

- Rotate the crystal/s. Do not forget to rotate the crystal/s you are cleansing during the sunlight cleanse. This is important in ensuring that the whole surface will get evenly exposed to the sun.

Full Moon Cleanse

This cleansing method is ideal whenever you feel the need to impart an incredibly intuitive, psychic, and feminine boost of energy to your chosen crystals. The moon, more specifically the full moon, has an abundance of divine feminine energy.

With that in mind, cleansing and recharging crystals in this light can greatly benefit you. To make the cleansing more potent, though, it would be best for you to do a full ceremony that runs overnight. This ceremony could also include candles, tarot, astrological reading, incense, a sacred plant, or another spiritual ritual that resonates with you.

To perform this method of cleansing crystals, follow the following steps and tips:

- Identify the best time to begin the full moon cleanse as well as the crystal/s you intend to cleanse and recharge.

- Look for a spot where you can put your crystal/s. It could be a ceremonial fabric, grass, or upon other crystals, like Amethyst beds. Make sure that you protect the crystals from other passersby, animals, and the weather, too. You may also choose to set the crystals inside a glass-based box to prevent them from getting damaged overnight.

- Start the ceremony. To do that, set the crystal/s in their specific place. Perform the sacred ritual such as tarot, if you have chosen to include one. After that, let the full moon bless the crystals with their power by leaving them overnight.

- The next morning, check the cleansed crystals. Ensure that they were not damaged nor dirtied during the process of leaving them overnight. Rinse them briefly beneath pure water.

This cleansing method is ideal for all stones and crystals, though it is particularly powerful when using it for selenite, opal, labradorite, howlite, and moonstone. Take precautionary measures when planning to cleanse stones and crystals that may get damaged by snow or rain through this method. Examples include selenite, kyanite, halite, and other soft stones.

Pure Water Cleanse

You can also cleanse the crystals with the help of pure water. You can use clean and pure water for bathing your chosen crystals regularly. It helps to use natural water sources, like lakes, rivers, springs, and streams, when doing the cleanse.

If you can't find the best natural source of water for cleansing purposes, use the water that comes out of your faucet. Make sure that you take additional steps that will help guarantee that the water becomes pure and clean enough, though, like filtering it, to remove unwanted chemicals.

To do the actual cleansing of crystals using pure water, these steps and tips can help:

- Look for the best source of pure and clean water that you can use to cleanse your crystals.

- Pour plenty of this water over the crystals. Just simply bathe them within the water for around one to five minutes. This step also requires you to massage the crystals gently.

- During this time, you might like to say some prayers and mantras. Make sure to hold the positive intentions you have in your soul, too. It can help in transmitting the required positive energy to cleanse and recharge the crystals completely.

- Use a towel made with natural fibers to pat down the crystals gently. Do this before you put them back in their sacred spots or altars.

- Express your gratitude for the work done on the crystals.

This method is highly recommended for cleansing only hard crystals, like jade, amethyst, quartz, rock crystal, onyx, agate, and carnelian.

Saltwater Cleanse

You may also want to do a saltwater cleanse on your crystals. Similar to pure water, you can also expect saltwater to be a powerful means of cleansing. This method is also famous for its powerful recharging capabilities. As much as possible, look for a natural saltwater source.

With that, you have an assurance that the water will be of supreme quality while retaining natural energetic properties. If you can't access a natural source, you can just use pure and clean water and integrate pink Himalayan salt or sea salt into it. You may also want to apply the salt directly to wet crystals. Just make sure to avoid using too much salt. Just a pinch in a bowl containing pure water is enough.

Here are simple steps that will let you do the saltwater cleanse for your crystals:

- Pour saltwater over your crystals.

- Let the crystals get submerged in it for a while. Just leave them there for a few minutes – max of five, in most cases. You may also want to sprinkle salt over your crystals and leave them for a few minutes.

• Use pure water to rinse the crystals, then use natural fiber towels to pat them down gently.

Just like when cleansing using pure water, the saltwater cleanse can also be expected to work well for hard crystals, like quartz, agate, rock crystal, onyx, carnelian, jade, and amethyst.

Other Ways to Cleanse Your Crystals

Apart from the aforementioned cleansing methods, you can also cleanse your crystals by doing the following:

• **Meditation or Visualization** – You can do this by sitting comfortably in a quiet and peaceful room first. Use your hand to hold your chosen crystal/s, then close your eyes. Let the serenity and silence inside the room embrace you. Visualize the crystal in your mind's eye.

Imagine that there is a bright white light coming from above that is pouring and shining over the crystal. Imagine this light washing away all negative energies present in the crystal. Continue doing this method until your intuition tells you that the crystal is cleansed.

- **Smudging** – You can do this crystal cleansing method with the aid of any herb you can think of. However, the most highly recommended herb is sage, as it is proven effective when it comes to cleansing the crystals. To do this, light up one white sage stick and then blow on it. You should be able to form a continuous stream of smoke.

Hold and wave the crystal in such a way that it follows the trail of the smoke. Your goal is to allow the smoke to rise and spill over your crystal. Do this for around five minutes or until you feel like the crystal has been successfully cleansed.

- **Brown Rice** – You may also want to use brown rice to cleanse your crystal/s. It is useful in drawing out the negativity within a contained and safe setting. This method works well for protective stones, like black tourmaline. To perform the cleanse, just prepare a bowl, then fill it up with brown rice.

Bury the stone or crystal beneath it. Make sure to dispose of the brown rice after doing the cleanse as it will have absorbed all the energy, particularly the bad and negative ones you intend to get rid of. This cleansing process often takes up to 24 hours.

- **Sound Healing** – You can also do the cleanse with the help of sounds. This method lets you use one tone or pitch to cleanse or wash over a spot, creating a vibration, which is similar to the tone or pitch. You can accomplish this through chanting, a nice bell, tuning fork, or singing bowl.

Sound healing and cleansing are perfect for collectors with numerous crystals that they can't easily move. It often takes around five to ten minutes for sound healing to work, and it is compatible with any stone and crystal.

Charging Your Crystals

Once properly cleansed, it is time for you to charge your stones or crystals. What you should do, in this case, is to put the stones or crystals on a piece of carnelian or clear quartz. You may also find sunlight useful as it can energize them. Put the crystal outdoors so it can get cleansed then charged subsequently by the sun. Charging them is also possible with the help of the moonlight, which is known for having subtle energy. This is great if you find the sun too intense for your chosen stone or crystal.

Other ways to charge your crystal would be:

- **With the Help of Other Crystals** – This means directing other crystals to the specific stone or crystal you wish to use. Form a circle with a few crystals, then put the one you wish to charge in the center. Let it stay in the center for 24 hours.

- **Surround it With Plants** – Alternatively, you may also bury the crystal in soil. Both methods are ideal if you prefer charging the crystal using the Earth's energy. You just have to put it in a garden so it will be surrounded with plants or bury it literally in the soil. If you decide to go for the latter, make sure that you put a marker on the area, so you will know exactly where you buried it.

- **Use Your Own Thoughts** – This means directing your thoughts to the crystal you want to charge. In this case, you can pray, chant, do focused meditation, or visualize your intentions, as all these are effective ways of directing not only your thoughts but also your intentions to the crystals. Just make sure to take your time when you do this. Note that the more effort and time you put into directing your thoughts, the better you will be able to charge the crystal.

- **Cast a Spell** – Another way to charge the crystal is to cast a magical spell into it. This is an effective way that practitioners of Wicca often charge their crystals with healing energy.

You may also want to make your own spell. Just think of the specific thing that you want the crystal to do. For instance, if your goal is to give it healing power, then put that goal to writing. After that, think of the things you have to say that represent that goal or purpose. An example would be making a rhyming poem that will serve as your spell.

Once you have the spell, just say it aloud with your hands holding the crystal. You may also like to do this spell while having a ceremony, like putting the crystal on an altar or lighting candles.

Programming and Activating Your Crystal

After cleansing and charging your crystal, it is time for you to program it so it can work in your favor. Note that even though crystals possess natural healing properties, it is still advisable for you to set an intention for the crystal or stone you have chosen. Doing so aids in connecting with its exact energy while restoring your sense of purpose.

You may want to hold the stone using your hand every time you meditate, as doing so can give you comfort. You may also want to put it over your third eye chakra. Another solution is to lay back while letting the stone rest on the chakra or body area you intend to target.

You should then visualize the energy of the stone or crystal merging or combining with yours. Speak to the crystal, either aloud or silently, and request assistance when planning to go through your present endeavor successfully. After that, express your gratitude to the crystal, especially because of its presence. You should then dedicate several minutes to meditate.

Just in case the stone or crystal feels like it is lacking its usual energy, you can greatly benefit from activating its energy a bit. One thing that you can do is to lend your energy to the crystal. All you have to do is speak or sing to it, or you can use your breath to send vital life force energy.

Another way to do this is to make an activation grid. You can do that by letting the more energetic counterparts of the stone or crystal surround it. In that case, your best choices for the counterparts are ruby, kyanite, carnelian, selenite, and clear quartz.

Chapter 7: How to Use Crystals for Healing

This chapter will give you a clear idea of how you can specifically use the crystals you have chosen for healing. Remember that before you ever use the crystals, you need to have them cleansed and charged first. Once you've completed both steps based on the previous chapter's guidelines, it is time to put these crystals to good use.

One thing to continue reminding yourself of is that all crystals are unique, which means that you do not have to follow a strict routine or set of rules when it comes to their use. Each crystal also has its own benefits that will somehow dictate to you how to use it, look after it, and maximize its benefits. You can also maximize each crystal's potential and effects by using the right approaches for cleansing, charging, positioning, and setting intentions.

Crystal Accessories

Undeniably, the ultimate benefit of crystals is their ability to heal you physically, mentally, emotionally, and spiritually, but it is also not a secret that these crystals are genuinely beautiful.

With that, you can take advantage of their healing powers by wearing crystal accessories or decorating your home and office with them. Apart from looking great, wearing and using crystal accessories as home decorations can help ensure that you will be able to retain positive energy within you and around your home.

Also, remember that crystal healing greatly depends on keeping your energy points or chakra system stable. Your body has seven chakras beginning from the crown found on your head down to your spine's base. In this case, you can use and wear a chakra accessory that you can buy from a legitimate website or crystal therapy clinic. This can be a big help if you want to target a specific chakra or ailment.

Crystal accessories you can use include:

- **Prayer Beads** – You can wear prayer beads made of crystals against your heart. Doing so can stimulate all forms of positive emotions, like peace, hope, and courage. Having the prayer beads around will also let you carry the power and energy of the healing crystals with you.

- **Jewelry** – You can also take advantage of the crystals' healing power by wearing pieces of jewelry based on them. Aside from healing you and showering you with positive energy, wearing their jewelry pieces also lets you show off the magnificent beauty of each stone.

- **Coasters** – You can also find coasters made from authentic crystals and gemstones. You can invest in these pieces and make them part of your home to embrace their healing power and positive energy. For instance, you can buy a coaster made of agate stone and make it part of your household decorations. This stone can stimulate harmony and balance in your home while emitting only good and positive energies.

- **Water Bottles** – Water bottles are increasingly being used alongside crystals. These water bottles come with a gemstone inside of them. Investing in these crystal-based water bottles can promote beauty, balance, and wellness.

Wearing crystals and decorating your home with them are truly effective ways to tap into their energy. Note that you will be able to absorb their positive vibrations and healing power even better if you touch them frequently.

The good news is that it is not that hard to wear and use crystals nowadays as they are often integrated into various items:

jewelry, clothing, beauty products, and home decor. You can just choose the most convenient method for you. If you are not fond of wearing crystal accessories and jewelry, then you can just put one or two of them in your purse or pocket. You can then use it as your touchstone so you will feel grounded the entire day.

Meditate with Crystals

Another way to use stones and crystals for healing is to meditate with them. This is also an effective way to connect with your chosen crystals. You can increase the spiritual energy you can absorb by meditating while holding the crystal. By doing that, you can connect with its metaphysical powers.

To meditate with the crystal, begin by holding it using one or two hands. Make sure that your eyes are closed while you focus on your breathing patterns. Here, you can start feeling your body sink deeply to the earth, providing a feeling of being grounded. One sign that you have already attained such a grounding effect is when you feel lightness surrounding you.

Remember that there will also be instances when you will be unable to feel something immediately. It could be because some crystals do not resonate that quickly with you. There are also instances when their effects are so intense during meditation that they can make you feel goosebumps. Remember that every stone and crystal will have a different effect on you, so it is advisable to experiment and be patient when using them for meditation.

Crystal Grid

You can also create a crystal grid, which is another effective way to take full advantage of the stones and crystals' healing power and energy. This method requires you to arrange and organize a few crystals to form a sacred geometrical grid. This helps to magnify the power of the crystals.

If you want to use crystals with this approach, then here are a few steps to adhere to when setting up your crystal grid:

- **Pick and Set Your Intention** – This should serve as the first step, as your intention needs to be at the heart of the grid. Once you have chosen an intention, write it down on paper. Fold the paper, then put it at the center of your crystal display. Alternatively, you can just continue thinking of your intention while crafting the grid.

- **Select Your Stones and Crystals** – Now, it is time to pick the specific crystals and stones you will include in the grid. Your goal is to pick crystals with unique frequencies that can imbue your intention with a specific energy. Spend time researching the stones and crystals that align with and support the intention you have set. You may also want to use your intuition when it comes to picking the crystals.

- **Pick a Sacred Geometry** – Keep in mind that various sacred geometry grids also have various meanings. With that said, you should decide on or choose a shape, which resonates with you. It could be a spiral, seed of life, circle, medicine wheel, infinity loop, or labyrinth. You can choose to print the shape or draw it. Alternatively, you can buy a cloth that has your preferred shape as its print.

- **Create the Crystal Grid** – With your intention in mind or writing, start putting the stones and crystals you intend to use on the grid. Make sure to begin from the outer part of the shape, then work in. Continue to think about your intention while mindfully laying down the crystals.

Put the last crystal at the center of the grid. This should be your master crystal. Once it is set in place, you can connect and activate the grid. In this case, connect the dots metaphorically by using clear quartz. Start outside and work your way in.

You may also want to use grid cloths if you are still a beginner in crystal grids, or if you find some patterns complicated. With the help of this crystal grid, you can manifest, lock in an intention, and maximize the positive energy and healing power of your crystals.

Put Crystals on the Body

Another way to take advantage of crystals for healing is to put them on your body. This approach has a completely different result than when you are just holding the crystals. If you wish to heal a certain chakra, choose a stone or crystal which corresponds to it and put it on the specific part of your body where that chakra lives. This can help stir the energy surrounding the chakra while elevating the feelings and emotions necessary for healing.

You may also seek the aid of an experienced crystal therapist to put the stones and crystals on your body. A good therapist is already aware of the different approaches and methods guaranteed to maximize the healing power of crystals on the body. If you choose to work with a crystal therapist, expect the crystal healing session to involve you lying on a table while the therapist puts specific stones or crystals on certain parts of your body. This is done to allow positive energy and healing to flow to that specific body part.

In most cases, your chosen therapist will put the crystal on a body part that suffers from an illness, then use a stone or crystal that aids in alleviating or curing the symptom. For instance, if you are complaining about recurrent headaches, the therapist will likely put a stone or crystal capable of alleviating the tension around and on your forehead.

Swipe the Crystals

The therapist may also swipe the chosen crystals over your body. In that case, they may use a pendulum that has the crystal on the end and swing it gently over your body. This specific crystal healing technique is the perfect approach if your goal is to eliminate an energy imbalance in your body.

In most cases, the therapist will start swinging the pendulum gently at your feet. They will continue doing so until a steady and evenly balanced swing on two sites is formed. After that, expect the pendulum to be moved up gradually over your body while retaining a similar swing pattern. Every time the swing gets out of balance, the therapist will remain in that particular body part until it neutralizes again.

Other Ways to Heal Through Crystals

Apart from the crystal healing methods already mentioned, you can also take advantage of the healing power of crystals by making them a part of your routine. You can do so with the aid of these tips:

- **Create an Altar with Crystals** – If you have an altar at home, then you may want to increase its earth energy even further by adding crystals to it. Your altar should serve as a specific spot meant for appreciation, connection, and gratitude.

It could be just a small table containing symbolic and sacred items – among which are the crystals. Make sure that the crystals you put there are only those that encourage positive feelings and good memories in you.

- **Incorporate Crystals into Your Yoga Session** – Put a few crystals on your yoga mat before starting each session. By doing so, you can build a tranquil and peaceful space that will inspire and energize you during your yoga practice. It is even possible for you to put a crystal or two on your body when performing yoga poses.

Conclusion

Using healing crystals may be confusing and daunting for beginners, but with proper guidance, you will be able to master the entire process. Hopefully, you have gathered all the information you need to start taking advantage of crystal healing. The most important thing to remember is that you need to set the proper intention and correctly align it with the crystals you are using.

Also, instead of viewing healing crystals as objects, you should look at them as living beings capable of vibrating their unique frequencies. With that in mind, you should focus on building a strong relationship with them. Serve, cleanse, charge, and take care of them. That way, you can also expect your chosen crystals to serve you to the best of their abilities.

I hope you have enjoyed learning about the incredible healing powers of crystals. I wish you the best of luck on your spiritual journey!

- **Invest in Home Decors with Crystals** – You can also fill your home with the healing power and energy of crystals by adding crystal-based decorations.

Large crystals can be quite expensive, but they are also attractive statement pieces capable of shifting the energy in your home. However, if you do not want to spend too much money on a large stone, then you can always opt for a group of smaller crystals.

- **Add Crystals to Your Bath** – You can also make use of your time in the shower or bathtub by placing a few crystals in the water you are using.

However, remember that you can't expect all crystals to work well in the water, so find out first if the one you plan to use is safe to come in contact with the water. If you want to detoxify, you may want to use shungite and add it to your bath. On the other hand, rose quartz is a great addition to your bath if you want to nurture self-love.

There are indeed several ways for you to use crystals for healing. If possible, make them a part of your daily routine so you can experience the benefits of crystals on a regular basis.